Castell Coch lies 5 miles (8km) from the centre of Cardiff, just off the main road (A470) to Merthyr Tydfil. Visitors should approach the village of Tongwynlais and take the main left turn (signposted), the gate of the castle being $\frac{1}{4}$ mile (0.4km) farther on the left. OS 1:50,000 sheet 171 (NGR ST131826).

GW00691625

(Illustration by Delyth Lloyd)

1

A Castle in the Air

Castell Coch is astonishing. It is a spectacular 'castle in the air' which was actually built; a pseudo-medieval stronghold made possible by the combination of the wealth and enthusiasm of a great patron and the vision of his architect.

As it stands among beech woods on a steep hillside, overlooking the valley of the River Taff, Castell Coch is one of the most romantic buildings in the British Isles.

'A party of Welsh damsels, under the ruins of Castell Coch', by J. C. Ibbetson, 1759-1817 (By permission of the National Museum of Wales).

Beginnings

The original castle on this site was built in the thirteenth century by Gilbert the Red, earl of Gloucester, to guard the plain of Cardiff to the south and the narrow Taff gorge against the Welsh. Some time in the fifteenth century Castell Coch - the Red Castle - was destroyed, apparently by mines and fire. The ruins remained standing for the centuries that followed, and a substantial structure with corner tower was shown in pictures by an eighteenth-century artist, J.C. Ibbetson. When the antiquary G.T. Clark examined the ruins in

1850 all that remained were the foundations, from which the ground plan could be worked out, and a few metres of the walls of the south-west tower. The place was no more than a picturesque ruin, a splendid spot for picnic parties from Cardiff five miles away.

Right: *A photograph of about 1875, showing the ruined thirteenth century castle during the early stages of reconstruction. A temporary bridge lies on the line of the main entrance.*

Below: *An aerial view of the castle, surrounded by its beech woodland, from the south-east.*

The foundations were faithfully followed in the nineteenth-century reconstruction. The structure seen today is the result of what a scholarly Victorian architect thought a thirteenth-century castle ought to look like.

Two Dreamers

In 1871 the owner of Castell Coch, Lord Bute, arranged for the undergrowth and rubbish to be cleared from the ruins and for his architect, William Burges, to carry out a survey with the idea of reconstruction in mind.

Bute did not need another castle, Burges did not need another job; but together they created this wonderful extravaganza.

Lord Bute

The third marquis of Bute could afford to rebuild Castell Coch: he was reputed to be the richest man in the world.

'ohn Patrick Crichton Stuart, third marquis of Bute (1847-1900) who, as 'riend and patron, commissioned Burges to reconstruct Castell Coch. A 'ortrait, taken from an original, by E. Trevor Haynes about 1886.

The founder of the family fortunes was the 'rd earl of Bute, the unpopular Prime Minister George III's reign, who married the heiress Lady Mary Wortley-Montagu. His son, the first marquis, improved on this by marrying two heiresses: first, Charlotte Windsor, who inherited great estates in south Wales which were owned by the Herberts, earls of Pembroke; and second, Frances Coutts, of the great banking family. His son married Elizabeth Crichton, heiress of the earls of Dumfries.

It was the second marquis of Bute, great-grandson of the Prime Minister, who consolidated the family wealth and turned his estates into a business concern. He, too, married twice and married well, but he also made his mark as an industrialist: he is still famous as the maker of modern Cardiff. The Bute estates in Glamorgan represented only a sixth of the family lands, and they were in a state of neglect at the beginning of the nineteenth century.

John, the second marquis of Bute (1793-1848), 'the maker of modern Cardiff', whose development of the docks consolidated the Bute family fortune. A portrait, taken from an original, by E. Trevor Haynes about 1886.

The second marquis set out to make the small town of Cardiff into a new Liverpool - a seaport to handle the coal to be mined from his estates. He invested with courage and foresight: the docks he built eventually yielded him a fortune from port dues, increased ground rents as the city grew and prospered, and to huge mineral

Cardiff docks about 1860, with sailing craft moored at coal hoists (By permission of the Welsh Industrial and Maritime Museum).

royalties from the mining estates. It was a long-term investment from which his son was to benefit. By 1900 seven-and-a-half million tons of top quality coal were being shipped through the docks: Cardiff combined with Penarth and Barry was the greatest coalport in the world.

When the second marquis died in 1848 the crowds at his funeral were greater than those at the funeral of William IV. His heir, John, was an infant only six months old.

John, third marquis of Bute, as mayor of Cardiff, 1890-91 (By kind permission of the marquis of Bute).

John Patrick Crichton Stuart, third marquis of Bute, was born at Mount Stuart on the Isle of Bute in Scotland in September 1847. An orphan from the age of twelve, he inherited thirteen titles as well as estates totalling 117,000 acres (47,350 ha) in England, Scotland and Wales - including the ruined Castell Coch. During his minority the estates were ably managed by trustees: when he came of age Bute had a personal income of £300,000 a year.

Lord Bute was educated at Harrow and Christ Church, Oxford. He was an intelligent child though quite unlike his father, being a scholar and a recluse. He had very wide interests: he was an historian, archaeologist, philanthropist, herald, theologian, mystic and psychical researcher. He mastered twenty-one languages and translated from several of them: his best-known writing was an English translation of the Catholic Breviary. Bute was baptized an Anglican and brought up in the Presbyterian Church. On reaching the age of twenty-one he shocked the establishment by becoming a convert to Roman Catholicism; this sensational incident was the basis of Disraeli's novel *Lothair* published in 1870.

Bute was obsessed by the past and with imagery and symbolism, which were part of his religious view of this world and the next. He was interested in Welsh literature and history, but regarded himself as a Scot. In 1872 he married Gwendoline Howard, the daughter of Baron Howard of Glossop and granddaughter of the duke of Norfolk, premier earl of England and the leading Catholic layman in the country.

In spite of his intelligence and the opportunities offered by his great wealth, Bute took no part in politics, though he accepted the office of Mayor of Cardiff in 1890. He continued to work on the development of the docks that his father had begun and the overseeing of his affairs, but his passion was for the medieval world. He took refuge in the past, and in 1865, when he was eighteen, he met the man who could rebuild the past for him: William Burges.

William Burges

William Burges (1827-81), from a drawing appearing with an obituary in April 1881 (By courtesy of the Illustrated London News).

The Burges connection with Cardiff was established by means of the London firm of Walker, Burges and Cooper, which was responsible for the East Bute Docks. Alfred Burges, one of the partners, was a successful engineer who made enough money for his son

The chapel at Cardiff Castle. Designed by Burges as a memorial to the second marquis of Bute (By courtesy of Cardiff City Council).

to have a private income, and pursue his chosen career, working for pleasure rather than profit. He was born in 1827 and, like his future patron, became fascinated by the more picturesque aspects of the Middle Ages. He was a great admirer of Pugin, the champion of the neo-Gothic style of architecture.

Burges, known as Billy, was brilliant if somewhat eccentric. He was talkative and jovial; very short-sighted, and never married, but he was only known as 'Ugly' Burges to distinguish him from J.B. 'Pretty' Burgess, the painter who moved in the same circles. He was well liked in the art world; his friends included Swinburne, Godwin, Rossetti and other leaders of the Pre-Raphaelites. He enjoyed alcohol and probably opium as well.

The 'Yatman' cabinet, a highly decorated desk/secretaire designed by Burges for the Yatman brothers in 1858 (By permission of the Victoria and Albert Museum).

Apart from his highly original work as an architect, Burges designed furniture, stained glass, jewellery and metalwork. His concern for the minor arts and their importance places him as a precursor of the Arts and Crafts Movement. He was perhaps the most gifted of the Gothic revivalists. He frequently travelled abroad, taking an interest in archaeology and studying buildings of the medieval period. He was a High Church Anglican, but had an aesthetic rather than a theological approach to religion.

Burges was absorbed by the thirteenth century; he was fascinated by pagan survivals in Christian art. When fashion and taste began to swing away from the Gothic style Burges did not move with them: he remained happy with the medieval. He produced designs for the new Law Courts in the Strand and for cathedrals at Lille, Truro, Edinburgh, and Brisbane that were never built. His most important built works that were constructed were Cork Cathedral in Ireland, his own house in Melbury Road, Kensington,

Tower House (1875-81), Melbury Road, Kensington, which Burges designed for himself.

Cardiff Castle, and Castell Coch. He also built a splendid house in Park Place, Cardiff, for the Butes' chief engineer (1871-80).

In Lord Bute, Burges found the ideal patron. His first commission was the rebuilding of Cardiff Castle, the Welsh seat of the Butes, a castle with Roman, Norman, and eighteenth-century elements. As soon as Bute came of age he commissioned Burges to work on Castell Coch.

St Finbar's Cathedral, Cork. Designed by Burges, construction work began in 1863 (By courtesy of the National Library of Ireland).

Perspective view by A. H. Haig of Park House (1871-80), designed by Burges for the Butes' chief engineer, James McConnochie (By courtesy of the British Architectural Library).

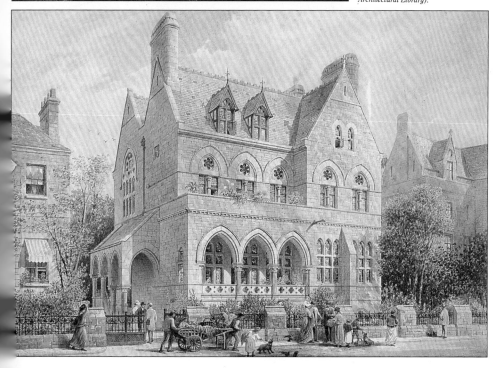

Castell Coch

In 1871 Lord Bute asked Burges, who was already working for him on the transformation of Cardiff Castle, to carry out a survey of Castell Coch and make proposals for its reconstruction.

Burges produced the *'Castell Coch Report'*, a fine album of drawings and plans now in the National Museum of Wales. He said that there were two courses open: to leave the ruins as they were or to restore them as 'a country residence for occasional occupation in the summer'. Bute accepted the latter alternative; but the project could not be a charge on the

estate, it had to be paid for out of his personal income. The Gloucester builder A. Estcourt was engaged and work began in 1875.

The startling turrets which make such an exotic silhouette were always controversial from the point of view of historical accuracy. Burges defended them as authentic, citing manuscript sources, continental examples, and the lack of evidence to the contrary. It is doubtful whether

I went yesterday morning to Castell Coch with Burges. I believe it will get on

Above: *Detail from a letter sent by Lord Bute to his wife in May 1876. He had just viewed work on the reconstruction with Burges and believed it would progress quickly.*

Below: *Detail from a page in Burges's 'Castell Coch Report' (1872). The top illustration is a view looking south through the courtyard, with the proposed Windlass Room to the left and the Keep Tower behind. The Kitchen Tower is to the right. The view below shows the castle as it existed at the time.*

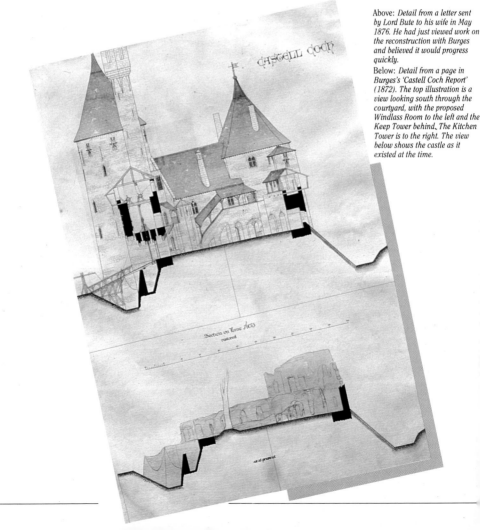

Chillon Castle, on Lake Geneva, Switzerland. Built largely in the thirteenth century, it was one of the sites upon which Burges drew for his reconstruction at Castell Coch (Photograph by P. H. Humphries).

the original castle had turrets anything like these, but the impression is magical. Burges was influenced by the Swiss castles at L'Aigle and Chillon on Lake Geneva, and by the work of the French architect Viollet-le-Duc at Carcassonne.

Billy Burges died suddenly in 1881, before much of the interior work on the castle had been completed. Lord Bute felt the loss of Burges intensely: their relationship had been that of allies and fellow-enthusiasts rather than architect and patron. Burges had been accepted by the family and had designed jewellery and other items for them. Lady Bute said of him:

In a letter sent to her sister in 1873, Lady Bute sketched a brooch recently given to her by Burges: 'I have drawn it as well as I can but my best is bad, it is really quite beautiful. . .'

The startling turrets at Castell Coch peak above the beech woodland.

'Ugly Burges, who designs lovely things. Isn't he a duck?'

The work on Castell Coch was completed under the direction of Burges's colleagues, William Frame and J.S. Chapple, who were loyal to Burges's intentions and, having worked with him before, were familiar with his attitudes and methods.

Whereas the exterior is a reasonably accurate reconstruction of a medieval castle, the interior represents the fantastic side of Burges's imagination with a riot of symbolism and decoration.

Castell Coch was finished in 1891, but it was scarcely ever used. Bute was more interested in projects in progress than in the final result. The stable block and offices were never built. A vineyard was established on the slopes below the castle. This produced wine for many years - the best of which went for communion wine, but in spite of Bute's interest in a Welsh wine industry the enterprise eventually foundered. The Bute children stayed in the castle when in quarantine with infectious diseases, but even the 'occasional summer residence' which Burges had suggested did not come about. Bute himself died in 1900. Since his death, Burges's red roof-tiles have been replaced by green. The glazed ridge tiles were originally by Doulton of Lambeth, modelled on one medieval sample

Retiling work on the Kitchen Tower in 1972.

excavated from the ruins. Again, it was necessary to replace these with modern copies in 1972. Otherwise there have been no major alterations.

A Tour of the Castle
The Exterior

The outside of the castle expresses the archaeological aspect of Burges's work. In most respects it faithfully represents the probable appearance of a thirteenth-century stronghold. The drawbridge, portcullis and projecting wooden bretaché over the entrance are as authentic as they could be. Burges drew on parallels at Caerphilly. Carlisle, Winchester, and the Tower of London in designing the details. The drawbridge can be raised, the portcullis lowered, and heavy stones, boiling water or tar could be poured through the murder-holes on to the heads of attackers. The

The only entrance to the castle is by way of a wooden bridge, the inner section of which can still be raised as a drawbridge on chains.

Beyond the drawbridge, Burges's 'defences' for the castle entrance included 'murder holes' and a portcullis which could be lowered (Illustration by Delyth Lloyd).

statue of the Virgin and Child over the entrance is by the Italian sculptor Ceccardo Fucinga, and was modelled upon one of Our Lady of Carcassonne. It is the only softening touch of decoration to the stark exterior walls.

Situated above the entrance is a statue of the Virgin and Child by the Italian sculptor Ceccardo Fucigna.

Purists may argue that dramatic turrets are neither English nor Welsh in character, but rather obviously French. Burges had to work hard to establish reasonable precedents for their shape, but who can regret a slight bending of historical truth to achieve such a dramatic skyline? Each of the three conical turrets is

The frontispiece drawing from the 'Castell Coch Report', showing Burges's original design for the reconstruction.

different from its fellows; the Keep Tower is the tallest and the Kitchen Tower is partly conical and partly pyramidal. In Burges's original design the roof of the Well Tower was intended to splay out over the parapet and a timber hoarding was to surround the top of the tower. This, in medieval days, was a temporary structure erected in time of siege to enable the castle's defenders to cover the walls below with their fire. The holes in the stonework to receive the timber supports can be seen in surviving tower walls in other castles. The removable wooden shutters, on horizontal hinges, were used to protect archers using the embrasures.

A covered gallery leads between the Kitchen and Well Towers. Removable wooden shutters are set on the outer embrasures, and served to 'protect archers'.

The imposing tower walls are ten feet (3m) thick at the base. The join between the original red sandstone and the nineteenth-century limestone can be seen part-way up the massive abutments. The austerity of the walls is relieved only by arrow-slits and drainage holes.

On the south side of the castle the ground falls steeply to the river valley; to the north there is a deep ditch. The only way into the castle is over the wooden bridge and across the drawbridge - the one could be burnt and the other raised when under attack.

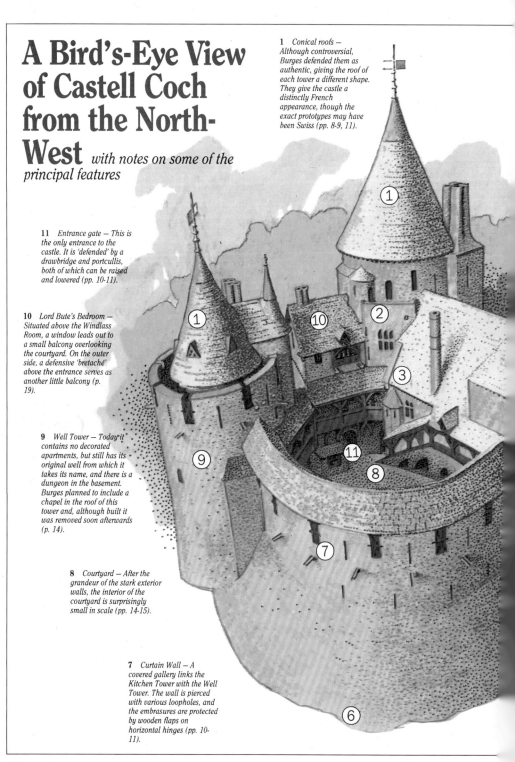

A Bird's-Eye View of Castell Coch from the North-West *with notes on some of the principal features*

1 Conical roofs — Although controversial, Burges defended them as authentic, giving the roof of each tower a different shape. They give the castle a distinctly French appearance, though the exact prototypes may have been Swiss (pp. 8-9, 11).

11 Entrance gate — This is the only entrance to the castle. It is 'defended' by a drawbridge and portcullis, both of which can be raised and lowered (pp. 10-11).

10 Lord Bute's Bedroom — Situated above the Windlass Room, a window leads out to a small balcony overlooking the courtyard. On the outer side, a defensive 'bretaché' above the entrance serves as another little balcony (p. 19).

9 Well Tower — Today it contains no decorated apartments, but still has its original well from which it takes its name, and there is a dungeon in the basement. Burges planned to include a chapel in the roof of this tower and, although built it was removed soon afterwards (p. 14).

8 Courtyard — After the grandeur of the stark exterior walls, the interior of the courtyard is surprisingly small in scale (pp. 14-15).

7 Curtain Wall — A covered gallery links the Kitchen Tower with the Well Tower. The wall is pierced with various loopholes, and the embrasures are protected by wooden flaps on horizontal hinges (pp. 10-11).

2 *Keep Tower — Originally planned to include six storeys, it was eventually divided into four rooms. It contains the two most decorative apartments in the castle, the Drawing Room and Lady Bute's Bedroom, each occupying two storeys (pp. 17-18, 20-1).*

3 *Banqueting Hall — This is a single range between the Kitchen Tower and the Keep. Burges placed the main hall on the first floor, with a plain servants' hall below (pp. 15-16).*

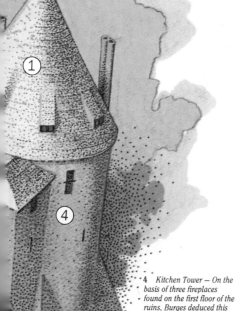

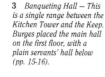

The highly-decorative ceiling in Lady Bute's bedroom (pp. 20-21).

4 *Kitchen Tower — On the basis of three fireplaces found on the first floor of the ruins, Burges deduced this had been the location of the medieval kitchen. Above the rebuilt kitchen the rooms are quite plain. There is an exhibition in the ground floor room (p. 14).*

5 *Spurred tower bases — These strengthen and support the Kitchen Tower and Keep. They are a feature of a number of late thirteenth-century castles in Wales and the March (pp. 10-11).*

Surrounding ditch — The ᵖ face of the castle, ₃g from this ditch shows ₃ strong the medieval ₃truction must have been 10-11).

(Illustration by John Banbury)

The Courtyard

After the forbidding grandeur of the exterior walls, the courtyard is surprisingly small, almost domestic in scale. It looks like a film set and, indeed, has frequently been used for this purpose. To the left of the entrance is the Keep Tower, then the Hall, the Kitchen Tower, the curved curtain wall, the Well Tower and the Gatehouse.

Beneath the Hall, a short flight of steps leads from the courtyard into the Servants' Hall. This plain room now serves as a shop. Beyond, in the far left corner of the courtyard, a door leads into the ground-floor room of the Kitchen Tower. A colourful exhibition in this vaulted room tells more of Burges and the background to Castell Coch.

The kitchen and the rooms furnished and decorated for the use of Lord and Lady Bute are all open to the public (The few rooms that are not open are empty and are generally uninteresting). The kitchen is plain and functional; the high chair is said to have been for the Bute children.

The Well Tower still has its original well, and Burges built a dungeon where he believed the original one to have been. This plain vaulted space has one nice detail: the light from the two tiny windows meets exactly in a square in the centre of the floor.

The ground floor of the Kitchen Tower now houses an exhibition covering William Burges and the background to Castell Coch.

A view of the courtyard looking south-east towards the entrance gate and the Keep Tower.

Burges's designs for this tower included a chapel projecting from the conical roof. Indeed, from a surviving photograph of the mid-1870s, this chapel certainly appears to have been partially if not wholly constructed. It extended over the edge of the tower and was supported

Two of the stained glass panels made for the chapel.

The panels are now displayed at Cardiff Castle (By courtesy of Cardiff City Council).

A photograph of the exterior of the castle taken in 1878. This view, from the north-west, shows the chapel clearly projecting from the roof level of the Well Tower (By courtesy of the marquis of Bute; photograph located by Mrs P. Sargent).

towards the courtyard on four stone corbels still to be seen in the walls. We know Burges had ordered the stained glass for the windows, but the chapel had apparently been removed by 1898. Possibly Lord Bute was unhappy with the finished work.

The Banqueting Hall

The entrance to the Banqueting Hall is by way of a covered wooden stair on the first floor. Here the reconstruction is purely conjectural, and we are entering the realm of high Victorian fantasy.

This hall is the first of what Burges called the Castellan's rooms, and is the least exciting. The ceiling, panelled with pine and cedarwood with designs stencilled on it, is supported by two fine king-posts.

An elaborate stone chimney-piece dominates the room. The central figure was sculpted by Thomas Nicholls and represents St Lucius, once believed to have been king of Britain in about A.D.200.

The figure of St Lucius, legendary king of Britain, situated above the chimney-piece in the Banqueting Hall.

Above: *The Banqueting Hall, largely constructed between 1878-79, with much of the decorative detail completed after Burges's death.*

Right: *Portrait of William Herbert (1508-1570), first earl of Pembroke, now hanging in the Banqueting Hall.*

The symbolism of the murals on the end walls, which were painted by Lonsdale, is obscure. The gruesome scenes apparently represent not very well-known early Christian martyrs.

The portraits are of the Herbert family, earls of Pembroke. The rather plain oak furniture was made by J.S. Chapple at the Bute workshop in Cardiff; the most interesting piece is the bench with a reversible back-rail. The fire grates in this room and the next were by Hart Son Peard & Company.

The Drawing Room

The octagonal Drawing Room shows Bute and Burges at their most exuberant. Originally it was planned as two rooms, one on top of the other; throwing them into one was an inspired modification. The splendid stone rib vault dominates the space, the gold lines of the ribs falling among birds, butterflies and stars in the sky. Below the level of the gallery vegetation begins: branches of monkeys, squirrels and foxes. Scenes from Aesop's Fables appear - the Hare and the Tortoise, Quack Frog, the Fox and the Crow, and others. The theme is Life and Death in Nature. The panelling of the lower part of the walls is illustrated by fifty-eight different flower patterns. The murals were painted by Charles Campbell of Campbell, Smith & Company a firm of architectural decorators founded under the aegis of Burges which still exists and has carried out restoration work at Castell Coch in recent years.

Round the doors are ingenious carved and painted mouldings of birds, insects and animals, inspired by fifteenth-century illuminated manuscripts. The tiles behind the fireplace embody the twelve Signs of the Zodiac. They are by W.B. Simpson & Son of London, who used blanks from Maw's tileworks at Ironbridge in Shropshire. Above the chimney-piece the statues of the Three Fates, daughters of Zeus, spinning the destiny of mankind, again are by Nicholls. The Fates surmount the Three Ages of

A detail of the wall decoration in the Drawing Room: Æsop's Fables — Quack Frog.

The great stone rib-vault of the Drawing Room, completed by 1887. Here, Burges explained in his Report, 'I have ventured to indulge in a little more ornament'.

Above: *Over the chimney-piece in the Drawing Room, the carved figures represent the 'Three Fates' of Greek mythology who controlled the destinies of men. Clotho spins the thread of life, Lachesis measures its length, and Atrepos cuts it at death. In turn, these rest above the 'Three Ages of Man'.*

A decorative detail from Æsop's Fables in the Drawing Room — The Fox and the Crow.

Man, and the rope - frayed and knotted - symbolizes Life. The three shields opposite are those of the Crichtons, the Stuarts, and the earldom of Windsor. The comfortless furniture

was designed by Burges. This work was all done, or at least put into place, after Burges's death, but his intentions were known.

Apparently hanging, from foliage round the walls, are portraits of the Bute family, starting to the right of the fireplace with the first marquis and ending to the left with the third marquis and his wife.

The Windlass Room

A short passage from the Drawing Room leads to the Windlass Room, where the mechanism for raising the portcullis is housed. Originally the drawbridge and the portcullis were to have their own counterweights, but this arrangement was simplified so that each acted as a counterweight to the other. There is a fireplace for 'heating water and other substances to pour down upon the enemy' through murder-holes in the floor.

Lord Bute's Bedroom

A spiral staircase leads to Lord Bute's Bedroom which is above the Windlass Room. This room is quite restrained when compared with the Drawing Room, although the walls are decorated with stencilled geometrical patterns. The furniture is chunky and even less comfortable than that in the other rooms. The most eye-catching feature of the room is a carved and painted frieze round the chimney-piece depicting endearing small animals among the brambles. Outside the window is a balcony overlooking the courtyard; as an inward-facing window it could afford to be large without making the castle vulnerable. Another spiral staircase leads to the Lady's Bedroom.

Detail from the carved frieze around the chimney-hood in Lord Bute's Bedroom (Illustration by Delyth Lloyd).

Lord Bute's Bedroom, completed in 1888, is contrastingly austere compared with the rooms below and above.

Lady Bute's Bedroom (1879-91), which in shape and decoration is pure Burges. The detail is rich in symbolism, but the dominant theme is undoubtedly 'The Sleeping Beauty'.

Gwendoline Howard, Lady Bute (1854-1932). A portrait, taken from an original, by E. Trevor Haynes, about 1886.

Lady Bute's Bedroom

This room, isolated within its thick walls, with small windows at the top of a narrow stair, is a world of its own. Here Burges's imagination has taken flight with French, Gothic and Moorish influences mixed with pure fantasy. The room was not completed until 1891, well after Burges's death, but it bears his imprint and is virtually untouched to this day.

The roof is a double dome with mirror glass entwined with brambles and thorns - the Sleeping Beauty motif. The winged figure over the chimney-piece represents Psyche, and the carved and painted capitals are particularly pleasing. Lord Bute apparently took exception to the monkeys on the wall as being too lascivious.

The room also has a lavatory in a small passageway within the thickness of the wall, romantically called by its old name of 'garderobe' by Burges. The scarlet and gold bed has fine crystal-ball bedknobs. Perhaps the most charming detail is the dotty castellated washstand, designed by J.S. Chapple, with hot and cold water tanks in its turrets.

The winged figure of 'Psyche', situated over the chimney-piece in Lady Bute's Bedroom, is typical of the symbolism seen in the decoration throughout the castle. 'Psyche', who, in Greek mythology, was a lover of cupid, is probably taken to represent the soul.

A decorative detail in Lady Bute's Bedroom.

The castellated washstand, designed by J.S. Chapple (1891), in Lady Bute's Bedroom.

Conclusion

The marquis of Bute seldom visited his dream castle after it had been built, and his descendants even more rarely. Castell Coch passed into the hands of the Department of the Environment and then to Cadw: Welsh Historic Monumnets. It is valued as a magnificant example of high Victorian Gothic architecture at its most exuberant, and as a fair representation of a medieval castle from an idealized feudal past.

For further information, the biography *William Burges and the High Victorian Dream* by J. Mordaunt Crook (1981) gives details of both the architect and of his remarkable patron. But Castell Coch is not so much a building to be read about as one to be seen and enjoyed.

Further Reading

J. Mordaunt Crook, *William Burges and the High Victorian Dream* (London, 1981).
J. Mordaunt Crook, *editor, The Strange Genius of William Burges 'Art-Architect', 1827-1881* (Cardiff, 1981).
P. Floud, *Castell Coch* (HMSO, Cardiff, 1954).

The Castle's Woodland Setting

The setting of the castle is as romantic and enchanting as the building itself: on the one side a sheer rock face and on the other a beautiful wooded hillside. The woods were planted for Lord Bute when the castle was rebuilt; oak, ash, sycamore, hornbeam and, above all, beech are now well established.

In this century the trees have largely regenerated themselves, but the apparently natural growth is, in fact, the result of a carefully managed programme of maintenance and planting that has been carried out in recent years. Over-mature trees are replaced by saplings; some of the sycamore is removed as it regenerates too easily and threatens to crowd out finer species; and there is a constant battle to stabilize the soil on the steep slopes. The soil is very thin and is vulnerable to erosion. Trees in this shallow soil are easily brought down by the wind, and when that happens there is a skittle effect which knocks down other trees leaving large gaps.

In May and June the hillside is covered with wild garlic — a plant that is supposed to ward off witches. The pungent smell of the garlic can linger on shoes and clothing for hours or even days. This garlic is the dominant flower, but other woodlands species such as celandine, bluebells, violets, lords and ladies, and dog's mercury, are also plentiful. Bluebells grow best in the woods on the hilltop, where many of the trees are draped in travellers joy (which is also called old man's beard). The woods beyond the castle grounds are in the care of the Forestry Commission and the walks continue through them. Over the top of the hill there is a long-disused mine, the 'blue water', which used to supply water to the castle and still does supply some local houses.

There are two quarries by the castle which, presumably, provided the stone for the original building. It is the iron in this limestone that gives it its reddish appearance. This stone was not used by Burges for the reconstruction as it tends to crumble, he used a purer limestone. The cliffs, which are now used for the early stages of training rock climbers, give added drama to the castle and would, originally, have been part of its defences.

These woods are now shared by foxes, squirrels, rabbits, small mammals, finches, nuthatches, jays and other birds, and by the human visitors who enjoy picnicking, walking, riding, and admire the majestic trees and splendid views over the Taff valley.

Woodland Trails

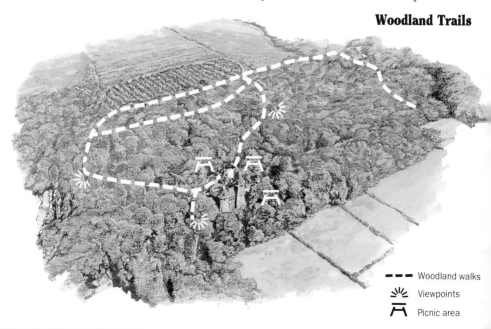

- - - Woodland walks

☀ Viewpoints

⊓ Picnic area

Castell Coch — Crynodeb

Castell Coch yw un o'r adeiladau mwyaf rhamantaidd yn Ynysoedd Prydain. Saif ymhlith coed ffawydd uwchlaw dyffryn yr Afon Taf. Yn y bedwaredd ganrif ar bymtheg yr adeiladwyd y castell sydd yma heddiw.

Hanes

Gan Gilbert de Clare, iarll Caerloyw yn y drydedd ganrif ar ddeg yr adeiladwyd y castell gwreiddiol ar y safle hwn. Cafodd ei ddinistrio rywbryd yn y bymthegfed ganrif a'i adael i ddadfeilio hyd ddiwedd y bedwaredd ganrif ar bymtheg pan gafodd ei ailadeiladu'n gyfan gwbl gan y pensaer William Burges ar gyfer y perchennog, trydydd Ardalydd Bute.

Yn ôl y farn gyffredinol, yr Arglwydd Bute oedd y person cyfoethocaf yn y byd — a chyfeirid at ei dad fel y person a fu'n gyfrifol am dwf a datblygiad Caerdydd. Yr oedd gan Bute ystadau yn Lloegr a'r Alban yn ogystal ag yng Nghymru. Ffolai ar y gorffennol yn enwedig ar yr Oesoedd Canol.

Ymhyfrydai Burges, y pensaer, hefyd yn yr Oesoedd Canol: yr oedd ef yn ddisgybl i Pugin a'r dull Gothig newydd. Dechreuodd weithio i'r Arglwydd Bute pan adeiladwyd Castell Caerdydd.

Ym 1875 y dechreuwyd ailadeiladu Castell Coch a pharhawyd â'r gwaith wedi marwolaeth Burges ym 1881.

Am Dro o Gwmpas yr Adeilad

Atgynhyrchiad manwl yw'r *tu allan* o gestyll y drydedd ganrif ar ddeg: mae'r bont godi a'r porthcwlis, er enghraifft, yn atgynrchiadau dilys. Ar y llaw arall, mae'r tyredau'n fwy dadleuol ac yn cario rhagor o ddylanwad Ffrainc na dylanwadau Cymreig neu Seisnig.

Mae pob un o'r tri thŵr, sef, y Prif Dŵr, Tŵr y Gegin a Thŵr y Ffynnon ychydig yn wahanol. Yn wreiddiol y bwriad oedd gosod byrddau pren o gwmpas brig Tŵr y Ffynnon. Ar eu gwaelod, mae'r muriau'n dri metr o drwch a gwelwn ynddynt dyllau saethu, tyllau traenio a thyllau gosod y sgaffaldau.

Fucinga, cerflunydd o'r Eidal, a fu'n gyfrifol am lunio'r cerflun o'r Fair Forwyn a'i Baban uwchlaw'r fynedfa. Eir i'r *Cwrt* drwy Dŷ'r Porth. I'w gymharu â mawredd y muriau allanol, nid yw'r Cwrt mor helaeth â hynny. Mae pob un o'r 'stafelloedd sydd o ddiddordeb ar agor i'r yhoedd.

Y Neuadd Wledda

Atgynhyrchiad dychmygol yw'r neuadd hon. Dyma fan cychwyn ffantasïau oes Victoria y ceir rhagor a rhagor ohonynt fel yr eir o ystafell i ystafell. Gan Thomas Nicholls y lluniwyd y cerflun o'r Brenin Lucius gerllaw'r simnai. Ni wyddys arwyddocâd sumbolau'r addurniadau a beintiwyd gan Lonsdale.

Yr Ystafell Groesawu

Mae'r ystafell hon wedi'i haddurno'n helaeth. Ar y nenfwd bwaog fe geir sêr ac adar, a hanner isaf yr ystafell yn gyforiog o blanhigion ac anifeiliaid o Chwedlau Aesop. Gan yr addurnwr pensaernïol, Charles Campbell y peintiwyd yr holl addurnwaith. Nicholls fu'n gyfrifol hefyd am lunio'r cerfluniau sydd uwchlaw'r lle tân ac yn cynrychioli'r Tair Tynged. Gan Burges y cynlluniwyd dodrefn yr ystafell hon ynghyd â dodrefn eraill yn y castell.

Ystafell y Wins

Yma y ceir y peirianwaith sy'n codi a gostwng y bont godi a'r porthcwlis; a phob un yn gweithio drwy wrthbwyso'r llall.

Ystafell Wely'r Arglwydd Bute

Mae hon ryw gymaint yn llai addurnol er bod y dodrefn yn drwm ac anghysurus. Ceir balconi uwchlaw'r cwrt.

Ystafell Wely'r Fonesig Bute

Ar ben y grisiau y mae'r ystafell hon sy'n fwy moethus ac addurnol. Amlygir yma ddylanwadau Ffrengig, Gothig a Mooraidd. Cynrychioli Gobaith a wna'r ffigur asgellog ar fron y simnai. Mae'r priflythrennau cerfiedig a beintiwyd yn arbennig o effeithiol. Ceir yma hefyd fasn ymolchi castellog a gynlluniwyd gan J S Chapple.

Hanes diweddar

Fel tŷ haf yr oedd y pensaer wedi'i fwriadu, ond hynny neu beidio, fu neb yn byw yn y Castell Coch haf na gaeaf. Bu farw'r Ardalydd Bute yn 1900, ac yn anfynych iawn yr ymwelai ei blant â'r lle. Daeth i ddwylo Adran yr Amgylchedd ac yn awr mae yng ngofal Cadw. Fe'i diogelir fel enghraifft nodedig o bensaerniaeth Gothig oes Victoria ynghyd ag atgynhyrchiad gofalus o gastell o'r Oesoedd Canol.

Tour of the Castle — A Summary

The tour suggested below follows the numbers marked on the adjacent plans. Page numbers in brackets refer to sections of the main guide with fuller details:

1   The visitor approaches the castle on its east side. The nineteenth-century walls and towers were built on thirteenth-century foundations. On the north and west the castle is surrounded by a deep ditch (pp. 10-11).

2   The entrance to the castle is across a wooden drawbridge. The gate is defended by a portcullis and 'murder-holes' (p. 10).

3   On the left of the courtyard, a flight of steps leads down to the Servants' Hall which now serves as a shop (p. 14).

4   Beyond, the ground floor of the Kitchen Tower houses an exhibition on William Burges and the castle (p. 14).

5   Leaving the exhibition, turn right and climb the steps to the gallery. The Kitchen Tower is along the gallery on the far left (p. 14).

6   Turn right out of the kitchen into the Banqueting Hall, the first of the castle's decorated rooms (pp. 15-16).

7   A doorway at the far end of the Banqueting Hall leads through to the richly decorated Drawing Room. The circular gallery above is not generally accessible and is best viewed from this point (pp. 17-18).

8   Leave the Drawing Room by the same door. Turning right along a passage, a short flight of steps leads to the Windlass Room where the portcullis mechanism is housed (p. 18).

9   The spiral steps continue up from this level to Lord Bute's Bedroom. The decoration here is restrained. The room is situated above the entrance and looks out over the courtyard (p. 19).

10   Continue up the spiral steps to the top of the Keep Tower. A short passage leads to Lady Bute's Bedroom, with its mirrored ceiling, furniture and views of the surrounding countryside (pp. 20-1).

11   Decend the steps back down through the Keep Tower. At the bottom, turn right through the Banqueting Hall out to the gallery. A covered section to the left takes you around the curtain wall (p. 11).

12   This covered gallery leads around to the plain Well Tower (p. 14).

13   Decend the steps to the ground floor, where the castle well is located. Left of the entrance a flight of steps leads down to the dungeon (p. 14).

A general view of the castle in its setting from the south-east.